NOTE TO PARENTS

Welcome to Kingfisher Readers! This program is designed to help young readers build skills, confidence, and a love of reading as they explore their favorite topics.

These tips can help you get more from the experience of reading books together. But remember, the most important thing is to make reading fun!

Tips to Warm Up Before Reading

- Ask your child to share what they already know about the topic.
- Preview the pages, pictures, sub-heads and captions, so your reader will have an idea what is coming.
- Share your questions. What are you both wondering about?

While Reading

- Stop and think at the end of each section. What was that about?
- Let the words make pictures in your minds. Share what you see.
- When you see a new word, talk it over. What does it mean?
- Do you have more questions? Wonder out loud!

After Reading

- Share the parts that were most interesting or surprising.
- Make connections to other books, similar topics, or experiences.
- Discuss what you'd like to know more about. Then find out!

With five distinct levels and a wealth of appealing topics, the Kingfisher Readers series provides children with an exciting way to learn to read and wonder about the world around them. Enjoy!

Ellie Costa, M.S. Ed.
Literacy Specialist, Bank Street School for Children, New York

KINGFISHER
READERS

level
5

Rainforests

James Harrison

KINGFISHER
NEW YORK

KINGFISHER
LONDON & NEW YORK

Distributed in the U.S. and Canada by Macmillan,
175 Fifth Ave., New York, NY 10010

Library of Congress Cataloging-in-Publication data
has been applied for.

Series editor: Thea Feldman
Literacy consultant: Ellie Costa, Bank St. College, New York

ISBN: 978-0-7534-6770-1 (HB)
ISBN: 978-0-7534-6771-8 (PB)

Kingfisher books are available for special promotions
and premiums. For details contact: Special Markets
Department, Macmillan, 175 Fifth Ave., New York, NY 10010.

For more information, please visit
www.kingfisherbooks.com

Printed in China
9 8 7 6 5 4 3 2 1
1TR/0811/WKT/UNTD/105MA

Picture credits
The Publisher would like to thank the following for permission to reproduce their material.
Every care has been taken to trace copyright holders. However, if there have been unintentional
omissions or failure to trace copyright holders, we apologize and will, if informed, endeavor
to make corrections in any future edition.
Top = t; Bottom = b; Center = c; Left = l; Right = r
Cover Shutterstock/Ammit, Nature Picture Library/Martin Dohrn, Nature PL/Phil Savoie,
Alamy/Edward Parker; Pages 4–5 Shutterstock/szefel; 5l Alamy/Frans Lanting; 5r Shutterstock/
worldswildlifewonders; 7tr Science Photo Library SPL/Jacques Jangouxl 10cl Alamy/Shorelark Nigel
Downer; 10–11b Photolibrary/OSF; 12 Frank Lane Picture Agency (FLPA)/Ingo Arndt/Minden;
13b Alamy/Bruce Farnsworth; 15 FLPA/Piotr Naskrecki/Minden; 16 Shutterstock/ecoventurestravel;
17tr FLPA/Frans Lanting; 20 Shutterstock/worldswildlifewonders; 21 FLPA/Piotr Naskrecki/Minden;
23 Shutterstock/Henrik Lehnerer; 24 Nature PL/Nick Gordon; 25 FLPA/Norbert Wu/Minden; 26b Nature
PL/Kim Taylor; 27b Nature PL/Kim Taylor; 28 FLPA/Frans Lanting; 29 FLPA/Thomas Marent/Minden;
30 Shutterstock/Colette3; 31t FLPA/Filip de Nooyer/Minden; 32 Shutterstock/Fikmik; 33t FLPA/
Imagebroker; 33b Ardea/Nick Gordeon; 34 Shutterstock/miorenz; 35t FLPA/Mike Lane; 35b FLPA/
Pete Oxford/Minden; 37t Ardea/Andrew Zvoznikov; 37b Nature Picture Library/Martin Dohrn; 38 Nature
Picture Library/Pete Oxford; 39t FLPA/D.Donne Bryant; 39b FLPA/Imagebroker; 40 Nature PL/
Phil Savoie; 41t Nature PL/Luiz Claudio Marigo; 41b Shutterstock/Frontpage; 42 Shutterstock/szefel;
43t Shutterstock/Dmitry Kosterev; 43b Alamy/Edward Parker; 44–45 Shutterstock/Frontpage; 45t
Alamy/Simon Rawles; 45b Shutterstock/Howard Sandler. All other images from the Kingfisher Artbank.

In rainforests, most of the wildlife lives high up in the treetops. This part of the forest is called the **canopy**. There is plenty of rain, wind, and sunlight to allow flowers, fruit, and leaves to grow and attract wildlife. The branches and leaves of the canopy can be so thick that they make the rainforest underneath shady and dark.

Macaws belong to the parrot family. They live in the Amazon rainforests.

Tree frogs have sticky pads on their toes to help them climb.

Where are rainforests?

There are tropical rainforests on either side of the **equator**. The equator is an imaginary line that circles the middle of the world like a belt. The tropics are areas north and south of the equator. There are no seasons there, and the weather is hot and wet all the time. The tropics give their name to tropical rainforests.

Nearly half of all tropical rainforests are in South America. The next biggest rainforest area is in Africa. Other tropical rainforests are found in Southeast Asia and Australia.

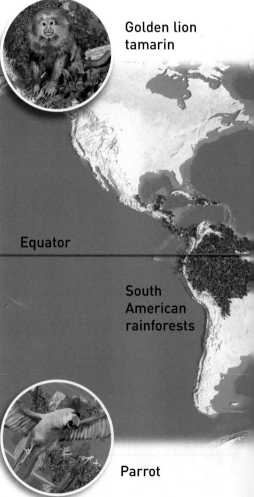

Golden lion tamarin

Equator

South American rainforests

Parrot

The tropics: This map shows the tropical rainforests (in dark green) in a band around the equator. The equator is halfway between the North and South poles.

The world's largest rainforest is the Amazon rainforest (pictured right) in South America. It is almost as big as the United States mainland. The world's biggest river, the Amazon, runs through it.

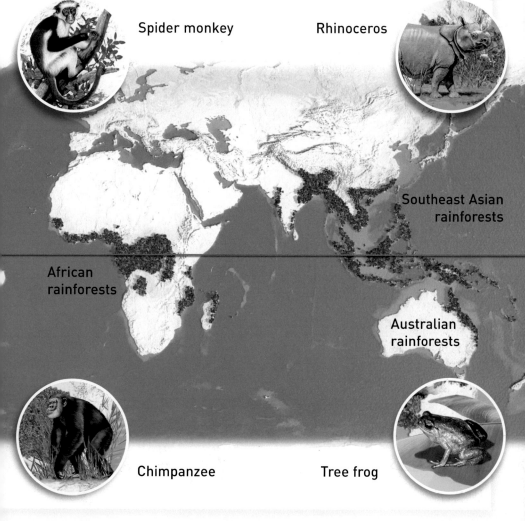

Spider monkey

Rhinoceros

Southeast Asian rainforests

African rainforests

Australian rainforests

Chimpanzee

Tree frog

Inside a tropical rainforest

Imagine you are walking on a soft pile of dead leaves in a dim light. You pass between giant tree trunks covered in twisted vines. Insects scuttle along old branches and dead leaves. There are a lot of ferns. You are on the rainforest floor, where it is quiet and still, as well as very hot and sticky.

Above you are the branches of small trees and bushes. High above them is the giant green roof of the forest. Very little sunlight, wind, or rain gets through this thick layer.

There are flocks of brightly colored parrots and groups of leaping monkeys. You might see a gibbon swinging through the branches. This is the busiest and noisiest part of the rainforest.

A tropical rainforest has
four main layers.

The emergent layer
This top layer
has giant trees
that can grow
well over 100 feet
(30 meters) high.

The canopy layer
Here there is a tangle
of branches, leaves,
vines, flowers, and fruit.

The understory
Leafy bushes and the
tops of small trees
make up this layer.

The forest floor
A layer of dead leaves
and mosses makes up
a soft carpet that is
ideal for insects.

Life in the treetops

The tallest trees in the **emergent layer** of the rainforest
tower 33 feet (10 meters) or more above the canopy.
At this height, they feel the full force of the rain, the
sun, and the wind. They have small, waxy leaves that
help keep them from drying out. The wind blows away
some of the leaves, but more grow to take their place.
Wind also helps spread the trees' seeds through the
rest of the forest.

The blue
morpho's bright
blue wings can
be 6 inches
(15 centimeters)
across.

Gibbons have long arms for swinging from branch to branch. They can travel 10 feet (3 meters) in a single swing.

The branches of the tallest trees can spread out as wide as a soccer field. They are the home of soaring eagles searching for **prey** and noisy gangs of high-flying parrots. Butterflies and bats fly in this top layer, and monkeys live there too. Gibbons are the only apes that spend their whole lives up in the trees.

In the canopy

The busiest and noisiest part of the rainforest is the canopy layer. It is made up of tangled leaves and branches. The leaves are mostly smooth and oval shaped and end in a point so the rain drips off them. Some sunlight, breezes, and rain come through the canopy, allowing fruits and flowers to grow.

In the tropics, every canopy tree releases huge amounts of water into the air. The moisture helps form the thick clouds that hang over most rainforests. The clouds keep the rainforest warm and damp.

This blue-headed parrot has green feathers on its body, wings, and tail. It has a high, squeaky call.

More animals live in the canopy
than anywhere else in the rainforest.
It is home to all sorts of monkeys—the
acrobats of the rainforest. Birds, snakes,
and tree frogs also live here. Many animals
can leap or glide from one tree to another.

Hidden world

Scientists know more about
the surface of the moon than
they know about the emergent
layer and canopy. They build
aerial walkways and fly in
hot-air balloons in order to
study this hidden world.

In the understory

The rainforest **understory** is humid, which means it is warm and wet. The understory is also dark because very little sunlight reaches it through the canopy. The plants here **adapt** to life in the shade. They grow large, dark green leaves to catch the little light that there is. These plants do not grow more than 13 feet (4 meters) tall.

Liana

Morpho butterfly

Yellow-banded poison-arrow frog

Lobster claw plant

There is very little wind, so plants rely on insects and animals to **pollinate** their flowers. There are more insects here than anywhere else in the rainforest.

Plants such as ferns and palms soak up the moisture on the forest floor. Lianas are climbing plants that grow well here too. They climb up other plants and trees. Many animals use them as ropes and bridges to reach the understory to look for food.

Vine

Tree frog

This diving lizard likes the warm, wet conditions of the rainforest.

The understory is full of small trees, as well as lianas, vines, and plants with large leaves.

On the rainforest floor

The forest floor is the lowest layer of the rainforest, and hardly any plants grow here. It is too dark for grass to grow. The ground is covered with dead leaves and twigs that have fallen from above. The largest rainforest animals, such as tapirs and capybaras, search for roots and **tubers**. Small creatures such as millipedes, scorpions, spiders, and earthworms find food here.

Many types of **fungi** grow here, helping rot the fallen leaves. The rotting leaves provide **nutrients** that the trees and plants take up through their roots to help them grow. All of these nutrients are in the top 2 inches (5 centimeters) of the soil, and they help the tallest trees grow in the very thin soil.

Tree frog

Mushrooms are fungi that eat or break down rotting trees and plants.

Trunks and roots
Some of the largest tree trunks are as wide as a car. Many tree trunks have huge roots called **buttress roots**. These stretch across the forest floor and take up water and nutrients from the soil to feed the tree.

Capybaras are related to guinea pigs, but they are much bigger—about 3 feet (1 meter) long.

Ants

Buttress root

Tapir

Not much light reaches the forest floor because of the thick canopy of leaves above.

Blue poison-arrow frog

A rainforest river

The biggest river in the world is the Amazon. It gives its name to the Amazon rainforest—the world's largest tropical rainforest. More than 1,000 smaller rivers and streams flow into the Amazon.

The main river is more than 4,000 miles (6,500 kilometers) long. It floods many parts of the rainforest every year and is home to some amazing creatures, including sharp-toothed piranhas.

Many animals eat the plants that grow on the riverbanks, but there are dangerous hunters in rainforest rivers.

Piranha

Caiman

Piranhas hunt in packs, and some **species** can be dangerous to humans. Other fish include giant catfish and electric eels that release a dangerous electric shock.

Long-nosed Amazon river dolphins search the muddy river bottom for food. Manatees are slow-moving **mammals** that browse in rivers, looking for water plants. They are also called sea cows. Alligators called caimans live along the riverbanks and in flooded swamps, snapping up turtles, fish, and even capybaras.

Capybara

Electric eel

Animals of the rainforest

The three-toed sloth hangs upside down from its powerful, hook-like claws and sleeps for as much as 16 hours a day. It may be the world's slowest-moving animal. The sloth stays in the trees eating leaves for most of the time and climbs down to the ground to go to the bathroom just once a week! Tiny plants grow on its fur and turn it green. This helps the sloth hide from its enemies, and its slow speed makes it difficult to spot.

This young sloth is gripping the tree with its claws as it climbs slowly upward.

Howler monkeys eat a lot of leaves and then spend most of the day resting. They move slowly, crawling up into the sunshine to warm their bodies after a cold night. Their deep howls can be heard many miles away.

Many rainforest monkeys and apes live high up in the trees. Some, such as gibbons, never come down to the ground. They live in large family groups, howling, shrieking, and barking. They are acrobats, swinging, gliding, and jumping from branch to branch. Most monkeys have tails that they use like an extra arm to swing around and to pick up food.

Beautiful birds

More types of birds live in the tropical rainforest than anywhere else in the world. One of the smallest birds on the planet, the bee hummingbird, lives here. It is about as long as your finger.

Hummingbirds can beat their wings 12,000 times a minute while they hover and suck out nectar from flowers with their long beaks. They are the only birds that can fly backward.

A hummingbird can stick out its tongue beyond the tip of its bill to reach the nectar inside flowers.

Scarlet macaws are very brightly colored. Like all parrots, they have sharp claws for climbing along branches and grasping food.

Beautiful, brightly colored parrots screech and flap in the canopy. Scarlet macaws are the largest parrots, and they have a 3-foot (1-meter)-long tail. They clamber through the branches to break open nuts and fruits with their powerful beaks. The largest bird in the treetops is the harpy eagle. Its wings stretch more than 6 feet (2 meters), and it can snatch a monkey in its strong claws.

Beaky bird

Toucans live in the tropical rainforests of Central and South America. They nest in tree holes with other members of their noisy treetop family. Toucans eat tropical fruits and nuts, as well as large insects, baby birds, and lizards.

The toucan's long, brightly colored beak is hollow. It uses it to reach fruit growing on branches that are too thin and weak for it to stand on.

A toucan's beak is made of the same material as our fingernails.

A toucan can even use its beak to pull baby birds from deep inside their nests and eat them. It can hold a nut with one foot and then use its strong beak to crack it open. A toucan's beak gets in the way when it flies, so the bird usually leaps from one tree to another with a few clumsy wing beats.

A toucan's huge beak
helps keep the bird cool.
Toucans (like other birds)
cannot sweat.

Insect armies

Thousands of tiny creatures such as beetles, ants, and woodlice scurry around on the forest floor, feeding on the rotting leaves and fungi. Many insects, such as ants and termites, live together in **colonies** that are organized like armies.

Leaf-cutter ants make an amazing army. They bite off pieces of leaves and carry them back to their enormous underground nest. There they chew the leaves thoroughly and then bring the chewed remains back up from their stomachs for fungi to grow on. The ants then eat this fungi. You could say they grow their own food.

The female worker ants carry pieces of leaves back to the nest to chew.

Worker ants carry the leaves. They are all female, and they work amazingly hard. Each piece of leaf weighs several times as much as the ant. The workers carry the pieces very fast over long distances.

So many ants

More than 50 different types of ants can live in an area of rainforest as small as 5 square feet (0.5 square meter).

King of the rainforest

Danger lurks at every level of a tropical rainforest. Animals on the ground must watch out for the biggest cat in the rainforest, the jaguar. The jaguar likes to prowl along tree branches, searching the forest floor for mice or larger animals such as monkeys, tapirs, and deer. This big cat moves very quietly on padded paws.

The jaguar's spotted coat helps it blend into the rainforest shadows, so it can creep up on its prey.

It swims and climbs trees well. A jaguar hunts alone and can hook out fish from the river with its paw.

A jaguar will even fight an alligator, and its powerful jaws can cut through a turtle's shell. These cats usually hunt at night, and they have excellent eyesight. Jaguars rest and sleep in the trees, often with a leg or tail hanging over a branch.

The jaguar hunts monkeys, such as this squirrel monkey, in the lower branches of trees.

Jaguars in danger

Jaguars once roamed the rainforests freely, using trees as cover. Today they are in danger of disappearing as rainforests are cleared. The animals are also hunted for their fur and by farmers who are afraid they will kill their cattle.

Hairy spiders and scary vampires

There are many strange animals in the rainforest. Tarantulas are huge spiders as big as your hand. The world's biggest spider is the goliath tarantula, which is as wide as a dinner plate. It is also called the bird-eating spider because it hunts small birds or young chicks in their nests.

Most tarantulas are black or brown and hairy. Many hunt using their sharp bite rather than spinning webs to catch food.

Tarantulas hunt at night. They are covered in thick hairs that sense their prey moving in the dark. These **predators** use their huge poisonous fangs to catch other spiders, insects, lizards, and frogs.

Jumping spiders can spring 50 times their body length in one leap, but they still get caught and eaten by tarantulas.

A thousand different types of bats live in the Amazon rainforest, but only one type feeds on blood. It is called the vampire bat. The bat hunts at night. It lands close to a sleeping animal and then walks up to it. The bat bites into the animal and then drinks its blood.

The hairy-legged vampire bat has very sharp teeth to bite into its prey without waking it up.

Other rainforest animals

Some of the strangest mammals **forage** for food on the forest floor. Armadillos have scaly body armor that protects their backs from big cats such as jaguars. Giant armadillos are as big as sheep. They use their powerful claws to dig for insects and worms.

The armadillo has a hard outer body armor made of bone that protects it from enemies.

Capybaras are the biggest **rodents** in the world. They are the same size as pigs and are related to guinea pigs. They have partly webbed feet, which makes them good swimmers. On land, they are awkward and waddle along like ducks. They live in groups.

Tapirs have a strange nose that looks like a short elephant trunk.

Tapirs are **timid** animals that feed on leaves and fruit at night. During the day, they hide in the understory. Tapirs swim very well and can stay under the water for many minutes to hide from human or animal hunters.

The ocelot is now endangered because people hunt it for its beautiful, patterned fur.

The ocelot is a wildcat hunter with sharp, scissor-like teeth. It catches frogs, lizards, monkeys, and armadillos. An ocelot tears its food to pieces and swallows it whole; it does not chew.

Rainforest peoples

Different peoples live in rainforest villages along the banks of the rivers. In these villages, local tribes live in the same way they have lived for thousands of years. Among the native peoples are the Kayapo and Yanomami Indians of the Amazon.

Yanomami Indians have shown scientists where to find useful plants for medicine.

Native peoples live in harmony with the rainforests— hunting animals, fishing in the rivers, gathering fruits, nuts, and insects, and growing vegetables in small plots. Their food, clothing, medicines, and shelter all come from the forest.

Parts of the tropical rainforest are flooded for several months at a time, so people build their houses on stilts. They cut down smaller trees to make dugout canoes so they can travel around on the water.

A Kayapo boy from the Amazon rainforest. The Kayapo Indians farm and gather wild fruits, nuts, and leaves from the forest.

Many peoples still take part in ancient ceremonies and wear face paint and bright, feathered headdresses.

More recently, other people have moved to the rainforest from the crowded big cities where it is hard to earn money. These people clear the forest so they can grow food.

Living with the rainforest

The people who have always lived in the rainforest know that the soil there is thin. They cannot grow crops for more than a few years on one piece of land.

People clear a small patch by cutting down plants and setting fire to them. Then they grow crops to eat and to feed their farm animals. They plant sweet potatoes, corn, and beans, as well as fruit and palm trees, but they leave the big trees standing. They farm the land for a few years and then let rainforest plants grow again.

This man is chopping open the hard outer shells to take out the Brazil nuts inside.

A woman picks ripe berries from a coffee bush.

Some tribes also gather wild fruits, nuts, and leaves from the forest and plants for medicine. They know what to look for and what to avoid. Some rainforest people sell what they grow and catch in markets, including coffee, cotton, and fish. They also cut vines and palm leaves to make twine, nets, baskets, and sleeping mats.

Rubber from trees
Many people work in the rubber industry. They drain a sticky, white liquid called **latex** from wild rubber trees. This is used to make things such as tires.

Workers cut a slit in the tree bark and collect the latex in a can.

Rainforests in danger

Large areas of tropical rainforest are destroyed every day. This is partly because companies cut down trees to sell as timber. The hardwood is used to make furniture and paper. Other companies clear areas of forest so that cattle can graze there, and then they sell the meat as beef around the world. Some companies destroy areas of the rainforest so they can dig out valuable **minerals** lying under the ground.

Many animals, such as this tree frog, are in danger of **extinction** if the rainforest is destroyed.

Today there are roads running through many rainforests. Giant trucks carry logs, minerals, and farm animals along the roads. People build towns for the workers who come to live there. Companies build dams and pipelines that may **pollute** the land and the water. Many local tribes are forced to leave.

Farmers clear the forests so they can plant huge fields of soybeans and other crops. These are fed to huge herds of cattle kept on even bigger ranches. Much of the beef from the cattle goes into hamburgers and pet food.

Rainforest trees are cut down or burned to turn the land into plantations or cattle ranches.

Rainforest resources

Tropical rainforests are home to a huge range of wildlife and plants—more than anywhere else on Earth. Yet rainforests cover only a tiny part of our planet. When rainforests disappear, so do the amazing animals and plants that live in them.

Tropical rainforest plants give us many medicines and drugs, including those used to fight cancer.

Tropical rainforests are sometimes called "the lungs of the planet." This is because the millions of rainforest trees and plants take in **carbon dioxide** and give out oxygen, which is the gas we need to breathe. Humans are pumping out too much carbon dioxide from power plants, factories, and cars.

A single rainforest tree is home to dozens of types of ants.

Too much carbon dioxide in Earth's **atmosphere** leads to **global warming**, which can change our climate. When people cut down rainforests, that leaves fewer trees to turn the carbon dioxide into oxygen. This makes the problem of global warming worse.

This pretty plant, the rosy periwinkle, is used to make drugs that treat some types of cancer. It grows in the rainforests of Madagascar.

Rainforest future

As you read this book, tropical rainforests are shrinking. Every second, a piece of rainforest the size of a soccer field is destroyed or damaged. The future of the world's rainforests is very uncertain.

Rainforests are cut down for timber and to make large farms to grow crops and raise cattle. Companies that mine minerals and build new roads, towns, and pipelines all destroy areas of rainforest.

Fair trade companies work with local people to protect them and the **environment**.

Today there are many **campaigns** to protect rainforests. One program creates **reserves** or parks where no one can build or clear trees to make large farms. Everyone can help rainforests by buying fair trade bananas, coffee, and cocoa, as well as wood and paper sold by companies that do not destroy the forests.

Rainforests need clean, flowing rivers and regular flooding to nourish the soil.

Rainforests are home to wonderful wildlife, such as the very rare golden lion tamarin.

Glossary

adapt to change in order to survive

aerial walkways tree branches in the canopy, or human-made rope bridges

atmosphere the layer of air around Earth

buttress roots roots that often grow from a trunk and help keep a tree standing

camouflage a color or pattern that matches an animal's surroundings and makes it difficult to see

campaigns actions taken by groups of people to protect things, such as rainforests and the animals that live in them

canopy the rainforest's "roof," or layer of high branches

carbon dioxide a gas that is released into the atmosphere. Cutting down the trees that trap the gas leads to global warming

climate the general weather in an area

colonies groups of plants and animals that live together

emergent layer the tallest trees in a rainforest, above the canopy

environment the surroundings in which an animal or plant lives, including the other animals and plants that live there

equator an imaginary line around the middle of the world, halfway between the poles

extinction when an animal or plant species dies out completely

forage to search for food

fungi living things, such as mushrooms and toadstools, that are not plants or animals

global warming a rise in temperatures on Earth that can lead to problems for the environment, wildlife, and people

latex a milky substance that comes from rubber trees

mammals animals that feed their young on milk from their bodies

minerals substances that are part of Earth's rock and soil

nutrients food that plants and animals need to absorb in order to grow and stay healthy

pollinate to transfer pollen from one flower to another, part of the way plants make new plants

pollute to poison the air, water, or soil

predators animals that hunt other animals, or prey, for food

prey animals hunted and caught by other animals for food

reserves protected places

rodents mammals with long front teeth such as guinea pigs

species a group of plants or animals that breed together to produce young

timid shy

tropics areas of the world near the equator where it is always warm and often wet

tubers swollen stems of plants that grow underground

understory the area above the forest floor where bushes and young trees grow close together

47